Here to Help

NURSE

Rachel Blount

Photography by Bobby Humphrey

W
FRANKLIN WATTS
LONDON·SYDNEY

Franklin Watts
First published in Great Britain in 2016 by The Watts Publishing Group

Credits
Series Editors: Rachel Blount and Paul Humphrey
Series Designer: D. R. ink
Photographer: Bobby Humphrey
Produced for Franklin Watts by Discovery Books Ltd.

Dewey number: 610.73
HB ISBN: 978 1 4451 4011 7
Library eBook ISBN: 978 1 4451 4012 4

Printed in China

Franklin Watts
An imprint of
Hachette Children's Group
Part of The Watts Publishing Group
Carmelite House
50 Victoria Embankment
London EC4Y 0DZ

An Hachette UK Company
www.hachette.co.uk

www.franklinwatts.co.uk

The publisher and packager would like to thank Dominique and the staff at Birmingham
Children's Hospital; the following patients and their parents: Halimah Akhtar; Mia-Lou Barnett;
Bobby Field; Keira Murphy Johnston; Ismaeel Kauser; Alice O'Donnell; Isaac Smith; Erica Taylor;
Hollie Walker.

Contents

Words in **bold** are in the glossary on page 24.

I am a nurse

I work at a children's hospital. It is my job to look after children and help them get better.

I work long hours and sometimes through the night, as the children need caring for all of the time.

Hello, my name is Dominique.

How do nurses help us?

Some children have an **appointment** to come to hospital. Others come in as **emergencies**. This means every day can be very different.

There are lots of people who work here as a team. Here are some of them.

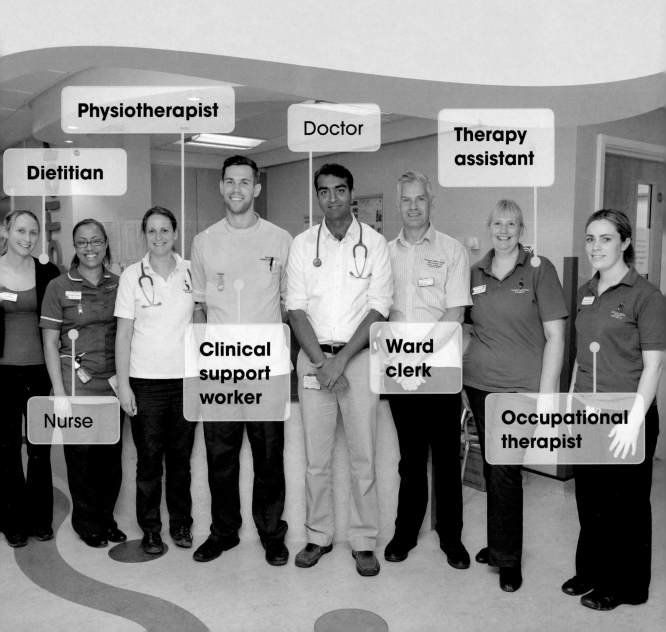

Physiotherapist

Doctor

Therapy assistant

Dietitian

Clinical support worker

Ward clerk

Nurse

Occupational therapist

6

Start of shift

I usually start work at 7:30 am. I meet the nurse in charge from the last **shift**. It is important that I know which patients are on the **ward** and if there are any problems.

Fob watch

Tunic

Name badge

ID badge

Hand sanitiser

I wear a dark blue **uniform** at work. I wear blue trousers and a blue top called a tunic.

Stethoscope – Sometimes I use a stethoscope to listen to a patient's **lungs**.

Name badge – This lets people know who I am.

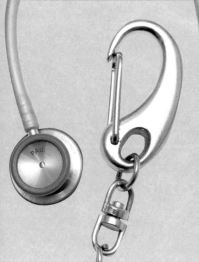

Birmingham Children's Hospital
NHS Foundation Trust
NHS

Dominique
Junior Sister

Fob watch – I use my watch to tell the time. I use it when taking a patient's **pulse**, too.

Why is it important for Dominique to keep her hands clean?

?

Hand sanitiser – This helps to keep my hands clean.

ADVANCED

HYGIENIC HAND RUB
GEL HYDRO-ALCOOLIQUE
POUR LES MAINS
GEL ALCOHÓLICO PARA
DESINFECCIÓN HIGIÉNICA
DE MANOS ANTISÉPTICO
PARA PIEL SANA
GEL ALCOÓLICO ANTISSÉPTICO
PARA MÃOS
ONTSMETTENDE HANDGEL
HYGIENISCHES
HÄNDEDESINFEKTIONSMITTEL
GEL TIL HÅNDDESINFEKTION
HYGIENISKT GEL

60 ml ℮   9650-641-EEU-F

On the ward

It is time to visit the children on the ward with Doctor Monaghan.

This baby is called Hollie. She is 5 months old and is having trouble breathing. Doctor Monaghan listens to Hollie's breathing with a stethoscope.

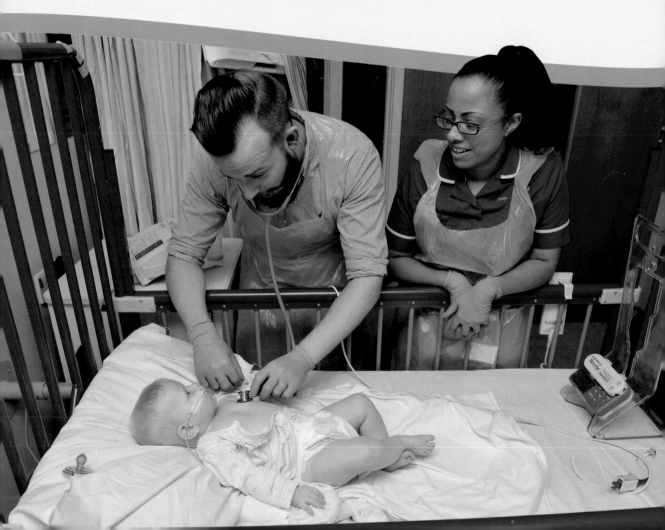

He writes in Hollie's patient **notes** and tells me what **medicine** Hollie needs. I will need to keep checking Hollie until her breathing is back to normal.

> **?** Have you visited a hospital ward? Why were you there?

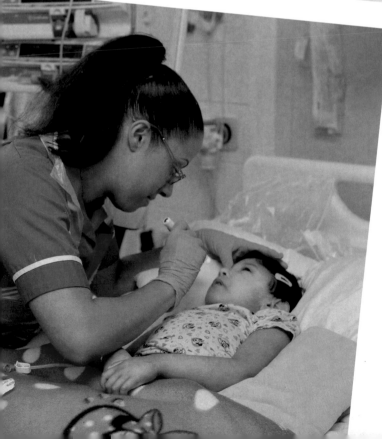

Next, I go to see Halimah. She is 5 years old. I check her eyes by shining a light into them. This lets me know whether her brain is working as it should.

Medicine

Next, it is time to give some children their medicine.

I wash my hands before I touch any medicine.

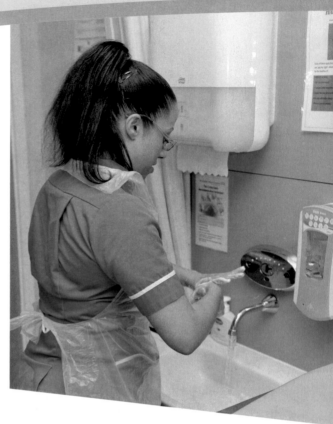

I get the medicine ready with nurse Asma. Another nurse always checks the type and amount of medicine for each patient.

?

Why does a second nurse check the medicine with Dominique?

This is baby Ismaeel. He has been sick and needs some medicine to make him better. Because he is so young, Ismaeel's medicine goes into his tummy through a tube in his nose.

Baby Alice needs to have her medicine through a tube in her arm. I place the **syringe** of medicine into the end of the tube and slowly give her the medicine.

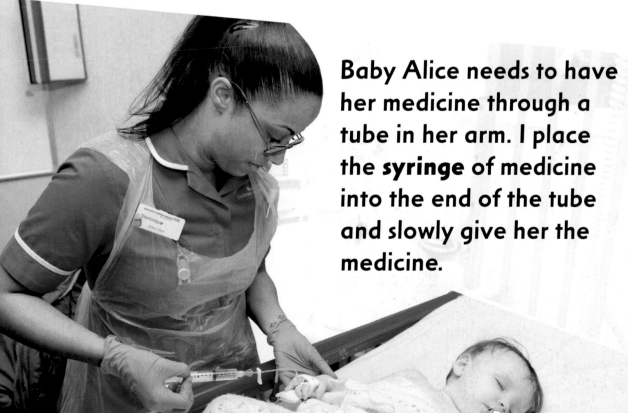

The playroom

I spend some of my time visiting children in the ward playroom. It is a place where children can come to play. This is important when they are unwell.

Hayley is a **play specialist**. She is playing with Keira to help her feel better about being in hospital.

I talk with Keira and ask her how she is. She tells me about her brothers and sisters. Keira wants to play some music for me on the keyboard. She is happy because she is going home today.

I'm looking forward to going home.

How does playing help children when they are in hospital?

?

Broken bone

Next, I chat with Doctor Charlie about a patient called Bobby. Her **X-ray** shows she has a broken bone where she fell on her arm. Bobby will need a **plaster cast** on her broken arm.

A plaster cast will help your arm get better.

Nurse Paul will put Bobby's plaster cast on. First, he puts a support bandage around Bobby's arm. Then he puts a special plaster on top of the bandage. Bobby chooses a bandage with hearts on it to go on top of the plaster.

?

Have you ever had a plaster cast? What did it feel like?

Nearly finished, Bobby.

Lunchtime

It's lunchtime on the ward. The catering staff, Kate and Brian arrive with the food trolley and get lunch ready for the patients.

I take a tray of lunch to Mia-Lou in her room. Some of the children have illnesses that are **infectious**. This means they can't be near other patients.

Here is your lunch Mia-Lou.

Children who are too ill to chew and swallow food have to be fed by a feeding tube.

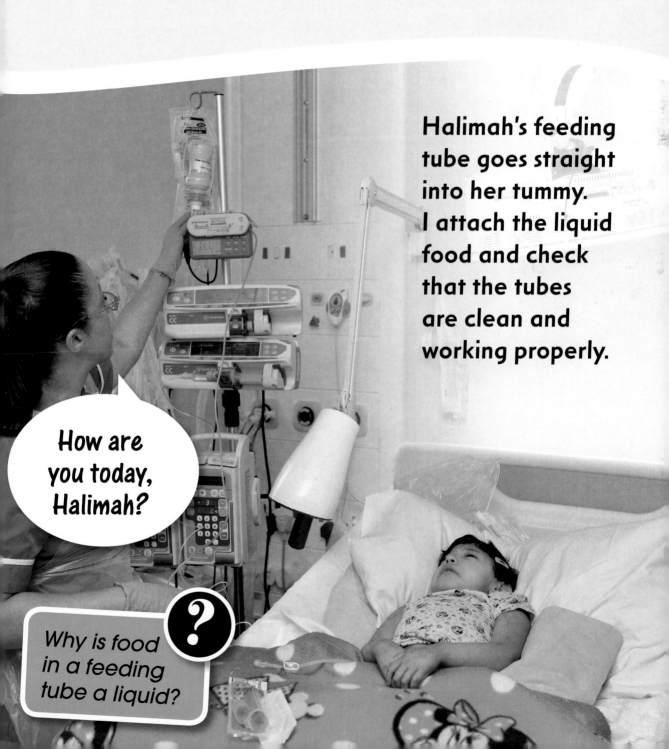

Halimah's feeding tube goes straight into her tummy. I attach the liquid food and check that the tubes are clean and working properly.

How are you today, Halimah?

? Why is food in a feeding tube a liquid?

Help to walk

I work closely with Jane and Eve from the physiotherapy team. Erica has had an operation on her leg and has crutches to help her walk.

Very good, Erica.

Jane asks Erica to stand on one leg. Eve stands behind Erica to support her in case she loses her balance.

Next, Erica has to lift her leg off the bed. Erica is working really hard today. The exercises help to make her muscles stronger.

You're doing really well!

Why does Erica need to do different exercises?

End of the day

It has been a busy day today. But there is still some work to do before I can go home.

I write up my notes on the children I have seen today. Then I check my emails on the computer.

Before I go I hand over to the next nurse in charge, Dawn. I tell her about any problems or children that might need extra help.

? Why is it important for the nurse to hand over notes to the next nurse in charge?

I walk once more around the ward to check all of the children. It is 8:30 pm and time to go home.

Helping people

I work with some great people who help me to do my job. Most of all I enjoy helping to make children feel better.

I really enjoy being a nurse.

When you grow up...

If you would like to be a nurse here are some simple tips and advice.

What kind of person are you?

- You're happy to work with people who are unwell
- You are kind and caring
- You are friendly and enjoy talking to people
- You enjoy working as part of a team
- Most of all, you enjoy helping people.

How do you become a nurse?

- You will have to achieve good grades at GCSE level in Maths, English and Science.
- You usually need three 'A' levels (SQA Highers in Biology, English and Maths) to get onto a university course.
- You can study for a nursing degree at university.

Answers

P4. Nurses help to look after patients when they are ill. They give medicine, carry out tests, make sure patients are clean and have everything they need to be comfortable.

P7. Dominique must have clean hands for good hygiene and to prevent infection.

P10. A second nurse must check the medicine to make sure the correct medicine and amount is being given.

P13. Playing helps children continue a normal, fun and enjoyable part of their life when they are being treated in hospital.

P17. Food in a feeding tube is a liquid so that is can flow well through the tube into the stomach.

P19. Erica practises different exercises to build the strength of different muscles in her leg.

P21. It is important for Dominique to let the next nurse know what the condition of each child is on the ward.

Were your answers the same as the ones in the book? Don't worry if they were different, sometimes there is more than one right answer. Talk about your answer with other people. Can you explain why you think your answer is right?

Glossary

appointment an arrangement to be somewhere at a set time

clinical support worker a person that works in hospital to support doctors and nurses

dietitian an expert on food and nutrition

emergencies unexpected and usually dangerous situations needing immediate action

hand sanitiser a gel or spray used on the hands to kill germs

infectious capable of causing infection

lungs two organs in the body that we use to breathe air

medicine liquids or tablets used to treat disease or relieve pain

notes written descriptions of a patient's treatment and medication

occupational therapist a trained professional who works with children with disabilities to help them become as independent as possible

physiotherapist a trained professional who helps people restore movement when they have been affected by injury, illness or a disability

plaster cast a bandage stiffened with special plaster to support a broken bone

play specialist a person who specialises in working with children using play, in a hospital setting

pulse the rhythm blood makes as it flows through arteries. You can feel a pulse in your neck or wrist

shift a set time when different groups of workers do the same job

stethoscope a medical instrument used for listening to sounds in the body, especially those of the heart and lungs

syringe a medical instrument used for injecting or sucking liquid into or out of the body

therapy assistant a person who works with and supports a physiotherapist

uniform special clothing worn by people who belong to the same organisation

ward a department within a hospital

ward clerk someone who works at the front desk of a ward in hospital

X-ray a special photograph of the inside of the body

Index